REFLECTING ON

The First Book of Homilies

with

Thomas Cranmer

Lee Gatiss

Scripture with the Saints
Reading the Bible with faithful believers across the ages

Reflecting on The First Book of Homilies with Thomas Cranmer
Scripture with the Saints

© Church Society 2025
Church Society
Ground Floor, Centre Block
Hille Business Estate,
132 St Albans Road
Watford WD24 4AE, UK
Tel +44 (0)1923 255410
www.churchsociety.org
admin@churchsociety.org

Unless otherwise stated, all Scripture quotations are taken from The Holy Bible, New International Version. Copyright © 1973, 1978, 1984, 2011 by Biblica, Inc. Used by permission. All rights reserved.

All rights reserved. Except as may be permitted by the Copyright Act, no part of this publication may be reproduced in any form or by any means without prior permission from the publisher.

Readers are reminded that the views expressed in this book do not necessarily represent those of Church Society.

Some of the studies in this book first appeared in *90 Days in Genesis, Exodus, Psalms, and Galatians with Calvin, Luther, Bullinger and Cranmer* by Lee Gatiss (Good Book Company, 2017).

Printed in the UK
ISBN: 978-1-0685705-5-1

'The dreadful ignorance as to the fundamentals of our holy religion, that almost everywhere abounds amongst the members of our established church, is chiefly owing to our neglect of preaching and putting into their hands the grand doctrines of the Reformation, contained in these *Homilies*.'

George Whitefield (1714–1770)

'The *Homilies* are a pattern of simplicity and godly sincerity. Never was truth more plainly stated than in them. In their mode of stating divine truth, and enforcing it upon the conscience, they never have been excelled by any composition whatever. It were well if they were more regarded as a pattern for popular addresses at this day: for, in comparison of them, the great mass of public addresses, if viewed with candour and with Apostolic zeal, would be found, it is to be feared, exceedingly defective, both in energy and in scriptural instruction.'

Charles Simeon (1759–1836)

Series Preface

> Remember your leaders, who spoke the word of God to you. Consider the outcome of their way of life and imitate their faith. Jesus Christ is the same yesterday and today and forever. Do not be carried away by all kinds of strange teachings.
>
> – Hebrews 13:7–9

The writer to the Hebrews encourages his listeners to remember their former Christian leaders who taught them the gospel and lived it out. We are urged elsewhere to honour our current spiritual guides (e.g. 1 Thessalonians 5:12–13), but here it seems to be former pastors that are in mind. As John Calvin (1509–1564) said, 'they who have begotten us in Christ ought to be to us in the place as it were of fathers', especially if they persevered to the end. So we are to imitate the way of life of these fathers in the faith and consider the outcome of their lives.

One good thing about learning from those who spoke the word of God and guided the church in the past is that we need have no fear that they will suddenly turn out to be rogues. Every generation has those who at a certain point swerve from the truth and upset the faith of some (see 2 Timothy 2:16–18). But we can see what the outcome of our fathers' way of life and teaching was, and how they served the same Saviour and Lord as we do today.

In an age which loves novelty, it is stabilising to consider the teaching and example of the saints who came before us. It can inoculate us against the strange teachings which vie for our attention in our own time, and help us to feed on more wholesome food. It can stir us up, correct us, rebuke us, and help us live out the unchanging gospel. This is not to commend superstitious devotion to the saints or romantic antiquarianism. Rather, it is to take seriously the charge to 'remember your leaders, who spoke the word of God to you.'

That's why in this series of short books we will be reflecting on the Bible together with trustworthy guides from church history who spoke the word of God. They will teach us, build us up in our ancient common faith, and bring the wisdom of the past into our daily lives. The word of God did not originate with us, and we are not the only ones it has reached! (1 Corinthians 14:36).

So I pray you will feel connected to your own spiritual family history as you sit down to study the Scriptures with some of the best guides from our past. They may see things in God's word which you had never noticed before. They may challenge you in ways you don't expect. And all they want in return is for you to follow Jesus Christ, who is the same yesterday, today, and forever – as they did.

How to use this book

Each day, this book gives you a passage of Scripture itself to read, and some questions to think about after you have done so. You will need your Bible open! It is good to reflect on what you have read in the word first, before moving on to see what others have said about it. Only after that will we have some guidance to ponder from our historical teacher. Their words are valuable only as they illuminate the unerring word of God itself and help us apply it to ourselves.

Following this, there will be some questions of application to think about. Spend some time meditating on how you can apply the word of God to your own life, in the light of what you have learned.

Finally, it is good to turn all this into prayer back to God. Spend some time talking to him about the lessons you learn in each day's reading. This will help you digest what you read and make it a part of your own walk with God.

There is a blank page after each day's feast, for you to record any reflections of your own, either in words or diagrams or drawings, as you feel led – whatever helps you remember and respond to the living word. What struck you most forcefully? What are you not sure about? What changes might this demand of you? How would you sum it all up? What should you pray for? In this way, this little book will also become a journal of your own daily dealings with God.

I hope you will feel invigorated, challenged, comforted, and urged on in your Christian life by reading Scripture with the saints. And most of all, that you will enjoy getting to know Christ better and growing in your love and appreciation for him.

LEE GATISS
Series Editor

Thomas Cranmer

Thomas Cranmer (1489–1556) was the chief architect of the English Reformation. Educated at the University of Cambridge, Cranmer rose to become Archbishop of Canterbury in 1533. He helped Henry VIII and Thomas Cromwell break England away from Rome, and established the liturgical and doctrinal framework for the newly independent and reformed Church of England. For this (and probably because he helped to build the case against Henry's marriage to her mother), the Roman Catholic Queen Mary had him burnt at the stake in Oxford.

Cranmer published the *First Book of Homilies* in 1547. It was intended to ensure that there was good, sound preaching in every Church of England parish each Sunday. Not all ministers were licensed or able to preach their own sermons, and so the Homilies were there to make up for this obvious lack, while efforts were made to train up more gospel preachers.

Not all of the Homilies were by Cranmer himself. The one on sin was by John Harpsfield (1516–1578), who was educated at New College, Oxford, and was a notable professor of Greek. The homily on love was from Bishop Edward Bonner (1500–1569), and the homily against adultery was by the Reformer Thomas Becon (1511–1567). But Cranmer was the editor and inspiration behind the whole collection.

Article 35 of *The Thirty-nine Articles of Religion* (still the legal doctrinal basis of the Church of England) states that these official Homilies contain 'godly and wholesome doctrine'. The great evangelical leader of the eighteenth century, George Whitefield (1714–1770), said they contain 'the grand doctrines of the Reformation'. The extracts here are taken from my updated and modernised edition published by Church Society.

※ Day 1 ※

No Stinking Puddles!

2 Timothy 3:10–17

The First Book of Homilies begins with 'A Fruitful Exhortation to the Reading and Knowledge of Holy Scripture', which urges us to read and love God's word, the Bible.

Read 2 Timothy 3:10–17

What does Paul say the Bible is?

What does he say the Bible is for?

A Satisfying Fountain

There can be nothing either more necessary or more profitable for a Christian than the knowledge of holy Scripture, since in it is contained God's true word, setting forth both his glory and mankind's duty. And there is no truth nor doctrine necessary for our justification and everlasting salvation, but it is (or may be) drawn out of that fountain and well of truth.

Therefore, as many as are desirous to enter into the right and perfect way to God must apply their minds to know holy Scripture, without which they can neither sufficiently know God and his will, or their office and duty. And as drink is pleasant to them that are dry, and meat to them that are hungry, so is the reading, hearing, searching and studying of holy Scripture to those that are desirous to know God, or themselves, and to do his will.

Unpleasant Truth

However, for those who are so drowned in worldly vanities that they neither savour God nor any godliness, their stomachs loathe and abhor the heavenly knowledge and food of God's word. For that is the cause why they desire such vanities, rather than the true knowledge of God.

When someone is sick with a fever, whatever they eat or drink (though it is never so pleasant), it is as bitter to them as wormwood, not for the bitterness of the meat but for the corrupt and bitter taste that is in their own tongue and mouth. Even so is the sweetness of God's word bitter, not of itself, but only to those who have their minds corrupted by being long accustomed to sin and love of this world.

Therefore, forsaking the corrupt judgment of carnal and worldly people, who care only for their physical carcass, let us reverently hear and read holy Scripture, which is the food of the soul. Let us diligently search for the well of life, in the books of the Old and New Testament, and not run to the stinking puddles of human traditions, devised by human imagination, for our justification and salvation.

Apply

Do you have a hunger for God's word, or are you 'drowned in worldly vanities'?

What 'stinking puddles of human traditions' are you tempted to drink from?

Pray

Thank God for revealing himself and his will to us in the Bible.

Pray for God to give you an appetite for his word, rather than for the pleasures of this world.

Notes and Prayers

✵ Day 2 ✵

The Usefulness of Scripture

Psalm 19:7–14

The Bible ought to be much in our hands, in our eyes, in our ears, in our mouths, and in our hearts.

Read Psalm 19:7–14

What do the words (laws, precepts, etc.) of the Lord do?

What would we be without the words of God, his commandments and rules?

Knowing God and Ourselves

Holy Scripture fully contains what we ought to do and what to avoid, what to believe, what to love, and what to look for at God's hands at length. In those books we shall find the Father from whom, the Son by whom, and the Holy Spirit in whom all things have their being and conservation; and these three persons are but one God, and one substance.

In these books, we may learn to know ourselves, how vile and miserable we are, and also to know God, how good he is of himself and how he communicates his goodness to us, and to all creatures. We may learn also in these books to know God's will and pleasure, as much as (for this present time) is convenient for us to know. And whatsoever is required for our salvation is fully contained in the Scripture of God.

Something for Everyone

Those who are ignorant may there learn and have knowledge. Those who are hard-hearted, and obstinate sinners, shall there find eternal torments (prepared by God's justice) to make them afraid, and to soften them. Those who are oppressed with misery in this world shall there find relief in the promises of eternal life, to their great consolation and comfort. Those who are wounded (by the devil) to death shall find there medicine, by which they may be restored again to health.

If it is necessary to teach any truth, or reprove false doctrine, to rebuke any vice, to commend any virtue, to give good counsel, to comfort, or to exhort, or to do any other thing requisite for our salvation, all those things we may learn plentifully from Scripture. There is abundantly enough, both for adults to eat, and children to suck. There is something appropriate for all ages, and for all ranks and all sorts of people.

These books therefore, ought to be much in our hands, in our eyes, in our ears, in our mouths, but most of all, in our hearts.

Apply

Do you come to the Bible just for stories and pithy words of comfort, or for the more serious tasks of learning, healing and salvation?

Do you think of reading the Bible as a chore, a massively useful exercise, or something else?

Pray

Thank God for revealing to us in the Bible our own situation before him, and the way of salvation.

Ask God to show you how comforting, healing and rebuking the Bible can be.

Notes and prayers

※ Day 3 ※

Building on the Rock

Matthew 7:24–27

The affection we have for the transitory things of this world will only be trumped by a greater desire for heavenly things if we diligently read God's word.

Read Matthew 7:24–27

What is assumed in both parts of Jesus's parable?

What is the real difference between a wise and a foolish man?

A More Excellent Treasure

The Scripture of God is the heavenly meat of our souls. The hearing and keeping of it makes us blessed, sanctifies us, and makes us holy; it converts our souls; it is a light to our feet; it is a sure, a constant, and a perpetual instrument of salvation; it gives wisdom to the humble and lowly hearts; it comforts, makes glad, cheers and cherishes our consciences; it is a more excellent jewel or treasure than any gold or precious stone; it is sweeter than honey, or honeycomb; it is called the best part, which Mary chose (Luke 10:42), for it has in it everlasting comfort.

The words of holy Scripture are called words of everlasting life, for they are God's instrument, ordained for that purpose. They have power to convert through God's promise, and they are effective, through God's assistance. Being received in a faithful heart, they have ever a heavenly spiritual-working in them – they are lively and mighty in operation, and sharper than any two-edged sword, dividing asunder the soul and the spirit, the joints and the marrow (Hebrews 4:12).

A Wise Builder

Christ calls him a wise builder that builds on his word, on his sure and substantial foundation. By this word of God we shall be judged: for the word that I speak (says Christ) is what shall judge in the last day. The person who keeps the word of Christ is promised the love and favour of God, and that they shall be the dwelling place or temple of the blessed Trinity.

Whoever is diligent to read this word, and in their heart to print what they read – the great affection for the transitory things of this world shall be diminished in them, and the great desire of heavenly things (that are therein promised of God) shall increase.

Apply

Since there will be troubles and difficulties in all our lives, are you committed to regular, careful reading of God's word, which is so vital for spiritual stability?

Have you 'printed' what you've learned this week from the Bible on your heart? How can you make sure you don't just forget what you've heard?

Pray

Ask God to help you build your life on his word, so your faith will withstand the assaults of the world, the flesh and the devil.

Ask him to help two or three of your friends to do the same, and to increase their desire for heavenly things.

NOTES AND PRAYERS

✷ Day 4 ✷

Sweeter Than Honey

Psalm 119:97–104

Whoever gives their mind to the holy Scriptures, with diligent study and fervent desire, will not be destitute of help.

Read Psalm 119:97–104

Meditating on God's word makes the psalm-writer wiser than various people. Who?

What is the result of understanding God's word?

Understanding Mysteries

If we lack a learned person to instruct and teach us, yet God himself from above will give light to our minds, and teach us those things which are necessary for us, and of which we are ignorant.

Many things in Scripture are spoken in obscure mysteries. Yet there is nothing spoken under dark mysteries in one place, but the self-same thing in other places is spoken more familiarly and plainly, to the capacity both of learned and unlearned. And those things in Scripture that are plain to understand, and necessary for salvation, everyone's duty is to learn them, to print them in memory, and effectually to exercise them. And as for the obscure mysteries, it is our duty to be contented to be ignorant in them, until such time as it shall please God, to open those things to us.

Making the Most of Our Privileges

In the meantime, if anyone lacks either aptitude or opportunity, God will not attribute it to their folly. Yet it is not fitting that such as are able to read should set aside reading simply because some others are not able to read. By Scripture, all are changed: the weak are strengthened, and the strong are comforted. So that surely, none are enemies to the reading of God's word except those who are either so ignorant that they do not know how wholesome a thing it is, or else are so sick that they hate the most comfortable medicine that would heal them, or so ungodly that they would wish the people still to continue in blindness and ignorance of God.

God's holy word is one of God's chief and principal benefits, given and declared to mankind here on earth. So let us with fear and reverence lay up (in the chest of our hearts) these necessary and fruitful lessons. Let us night and day muse, meditate, and contemplate them. Let us ruminate, and (as it were) chew the cud, that we may have the sweet juice, spiritual effect, honey, kernel, taste, comfort, and consolation of them.

Apply

What should we do when we come across parts of the Bible that we find difficult to understand?

How could you be more diligent and fervent in your study of God's precious word?

Pray

Thank God for the great and special gift of his word, which brings light and comfort to us.

Ask God to help you unravel and enjoy the parts of the Bible which you have found most difficult to understand or obey recently.

NOTES AND PRAYERS

✻ Day 5 ✻

The Misery of Humanity

Romans 3:9–20

God knows best what we are, and what we ought to be called. 'There is no one righteous, not even one.'

Read Romans 3:9–20

Are some people better than others in God's eyes?

How can we find out how sinful we are?

We Are Dust

The Holy Spirit, in writing the holy Scripture, is in nothing more diligent than to pull down man's vainglory and pride which, of all vices, is most universally grafted in all mankind. And therefore we read in many places of Scripture many notable lessons against this old rooted vice, to teach us the most commendable virtue of humility, how to know ourselves, and to remember what we are of ourselves.

In the book of Genesis, Almighty God gives us all a title and name in our great grandfather Adam, which ought to admonish us all to consider what we are, and where we came from. He says, 'By the sweat of your brow you will eat your food until you return to the ground, since from it you were taken; for dust you are and to dust you will return' (Genesis 3:19). Here (as in a mirror) we may learn to know ourselves to be but ground, earth and ashes—and that to earth and ashes we shall return.

It is not without great cause that the Scripture of God so many times calls all of us here in this world by this word: 'earth'. 'O earth, earth, earth' says Jeremiah, 'hear the word of the Lord' (Jeremiah 22:29, KJV). This our right name, vocation, and title – 'earth, earth, earth' – pronounced by the prophet, shows what we are indeed, regardless of whatever style, title or dignity people might use to describe us. Thus he who knows best plainly named us, both what we are and what we ought of right to be called.

Sinners by Nature

The Scripture shuts up all under sin, that the promise by the faith of Jesus Christ should be given to those who believe. The Apostle Paul in many places paints us in our true colours, calling us the 'children of [the] wrath [of God]' when we are born (Ephesians 2:3, ESV), saying also that we cannot think a good thought of ourselves, much less speak well or do well of ourselves. And the wise man says in the book of Proverbs, 'The righteous fall seven times' (Proverbs 24:16).

Apply

What would you say to someone who claimed that people are basically good on the inside?

Ponder what would happen to the world if God left us entirely to our own devices and desires.

Pray

Ask God for the 'most commendable virtue of humility': to know yourself truly.

Pray for his forgiveness for ways in which you have erred and strayed like a lost sheep.

Notes and Prayers

✳ Day 6 ✳

We Are Not Worthy

1 John 1:5–10

We learn from all good men in holy Scripture to humble ourselves, and to exalt, extol, praise, magnify and glorify God.

Read 1 John 1:5–10

What does John say about those who don't acknowledge their sin?

What is the best way to deal with sin, according to John?

Fruitless Trees

Few of the proud, just, learned, wise, perfect and holy Pharisees were saved by Jesus, because they justified themselves by their counterfeit holiness before people. Therefore, let us beware of such hypocrisy, vainglory and justifying of ourselves. Let us look at our feet, and then down peacock's feathers, down proud heart, down vile clay, frail and brittle vessels!

Of ourselves, we are crabtrees that can bring forth no apples. We are, of ourselves, of such earth, as can bring forth only weeds, nettles, brambles and briers. We have neither faith, love, hope, patience, chastity, nor anything else that is good, except from God. And therefore, these virtues are called in Galatians 5, the fruit of the Holy Spirit, and not the fruit of mankind.

Imperfect and Unworthy

Let us, therefore, acknowledge ourselves before God to be miserable and wretched sinners. And let us earnestly repent, and humble ourselves heartily, and cry to God for mercy. Let us know our own works, how imperfect they are, and then we shall not stand foolishly and arrogantly in our own conceits, nor think we can be justified by our merits or works.

For truly, there are imperfections in our best works. We do not love God as much as we are bound to do – with all our heart, mind and power. We do not fear God as much as we ought to do. We do not pray to God, but with great and many imperfections. We give, forgive, believe, live and hope imperfectly. We speak, think and do imperfectly. We fight against the devil, the world and the flesh imperfectly. Let us, therefore, not be ashamed to confess plainly our state of imperfection. Indeed, let us not be ashamed to confess imperfection, even in all our own best works.

Let none of us be ashamed, to say with the apostle Peter, 'I am a sinful man' (Luke 5:8). Let us all make open confession with the prodigal son to our father (Luke 15:18–19), and say with him, 'Father, we have sinned against heaven and against you. We are not worthy to be called your children'.

Apply

How does it make you feel that, by nature, you are not 'worthy' to be God's child?

What would you say to a non-Christian friend who says, 'I do my best to live a good life – surely God will be happy with that'?

Pray

Ask forgiveness for the times when you have 'followed too much the devices and desires of your own heart' (as the *Book of Common Prayer* puts it) this week.

Praise God that though we are more sinful than we could even imagine, he is more merciful than we could possibly dream.

Notes and Prayers

✴ Day 7 ✴

In Christ Alone

Ephesians 2:1–5

As of ourselves comes all evil and damnation, so likewise of God alone comes all goodness and salvation.

Read Ephesians 2:1–5

Who did we follow and obey, when we were dead in our sins (verses 2–3)?

Why did God make us alive and save us (verses 4–5)?

No Glory or Rejoicing in Ourselves

We have heard how evil we are of ourselves, and how of ourselves and by ourselves we have no goodness, help, or salvation – but rather, on the contrary, sin, damnation, and death everlasting. If we deeply weigh and consider this, we shall better understand the great mercy of God, and how our salvation comes only by Christ.

For in ourselves we find nothing by which we may be delivered from this miserable captivity into which we were cast, through the envy of the devil, by transgressing God's commandment in our first parent Adam. We have all become unclean, but we all are not able to cleanse ourselves, nor to make each other clean. We are by nature children of God's wrath, but we are not able to make ourselves the children and inheritors of God's glory. We are sheep that have gone astray, but we cannot of our own power come again to the sheepfold, so great is our imperfection and weakness.

We may not glory in ourselves, therefore, since of ourselves we are nothing but sinful. Neither may we rejoice in any works that we do, which are all so imperfect and impure that they are not able to stand before the righteous throne of God. As the holy prophet David says, 'Do not bring your servant into judgment, for no one living is righteous before you' (Psalm 143:2).

Rejoice in Christ Alone

To God, therefore, we must flee, or else we shall never find peace, rest and quietness of conscience in our hearts. For he is the Father of mercies, and God of all consolation.

O how much are we bound to our heavenly Father, for his great mercies, which he has so plenteously declared to us in Christ Jesus our Lord and Saviour! What thanks worthy and sufficient can we give to him? Let us all with one accord burst out with joyful voices, ever praising and magnifying this Lord of mercy for his tender kindness shown to us in his dearly beloved Son!

Apply

Let us learn to know ourselves, our frailty and weakness, without any ostentation or boasting of our own good deeds and merits.

Let us also acknowledge the exceedingly great mercy of God towards us, which we don't deserve.

Pray

Confess to God how you have left undone those things which you ought to have done, and done those things which you ought not to have done.

Praise him for his mercy and grace towards you in Christ, despite your sin.

Notes and prayers

❊ Day 8 ❊

The Wrath of God Was Satisfied

Romans 3:21–26

Although justification is by faith alone and free to us, yet it was not achieved without the payment of a ransom.

Read Romans 3:21–26

What did God do to enable us to be redeemed, despite our sin?

How can it be right for God to say that I'm in the right when I'm not?

Making Amends for Us

No one can by their own acts, works and deeds be justified, and made righteous before God. But everyone of necessity is constrained to seek for another righteousness, or justification, to be received at God's own hands – that is to say, the remission, pardon, and forgiveness of sins and trespasses, in such things as we have offended.

And this justification or righteousness, which we so receive by God's mercy and Christ's merits, embraced by faith, is taken, accepted and allowed of God, for our perfect and full justification. It is our duty ever to remember the great mercy of God, how (all the world being wrapped in sin, by breaking of the law) God sent his only Son, our Saviour Christ into this world, to fulfil the law for us; and by shedding of his most precious blood, to make a sacrifice and satisfaction or to make amends to his Father for our sins – to satisfy his wrath and indignation conceived against us because of them.

Justice and Mercy Embrace

In this mystery of our redemption, by the great wisdom of God, he has so tempered his justice and mercy together that he would neither by his justice condemn us unto the perpetual captivity of the devil and his prison of hell – remediless for ever without mercy – nor by his mercy deliver us clearly without justice, or payment of a just ransom. But with his endless mercy, he joined his most upright and equal justice.

His great mercy he showed to us in delivering us from our former captivity, without requiring any ransom to be paid or amends to be made on our part – which it would have been impossible for us to do. And since we did not have it in us to do so, he provided a ransom for us – the most precious body and blood of his own most dear and best beloved Son, Jesus Christ, who besides his ransom, fulfilled the law for us perfectly. And so the justice of God and his mercy did embrace together, and fulfilled the mystery of our redemption.

Apply

When you rejoice in the fact that salvation is by grace alone, never forget that what is freely given to us was bought with the precious blood of Christ.

Remember that God did not indulgently set aside his justice in order to save us, but fulfilled it.

Pray

Rejoice that Jesus bore the wrath of God for our sins, so that we don't have to.

Thank God that he is not merely the God of perfect justice, but also the God of endless mercy.

Notes and Prayers

✵ Day 9 ✵

Christ for Us

Romans 8:1–4

All the good works that we can do are unable to earn our salvation, which comes freely by the mere mercy of God because of Christ's work on our behalf.

Read Romans 8:1–4

What do we contribute to our salvation?

How can you be saved if you haven't fulfilled the law?

Faith and Works

Three things must concur and go together in our justification. First, on God's part, his great mercy and grace. Second, on Christ's part, justice – that is, the satisfaction of God's justice, or the price of our redemption by the offering of his body and shedding of his blood, with fulfilling of the law, perfectly and thoroughly. And third, on our part, true and lively faith in the merits of Jesus Christ, which yet is not ours, but by God's working in us.

Paul declares here nothing upon our behalf concerning our justification, but only a true and lively faith, which nevertheless is the gift of God. And yet that faith does not exclude repentance, hope, love, dread and the fear of God; these things are joined with faith in everyone who is justified. But although they are all present together in the one who is justified, yet they do not all justify together.

Nor does faith exclude the justice of our good works, necessarily to be done afterwards of duty towards God. For we are clearly bound to serve God in doing good deeds commanded by him in his holy Scripture, all the days of our life. But works are excluded from faith, in the sense that we may not do them in order to be made good by doing them.

The Precious Jewels

Our justification comes freely, by the mere mercy of God. We need such great and free mercy because no one in the whole world is able of themselves to pay any part towards their ransom. And yet it pleased our heavenly Father, of his infinite mercy, without any desert or deserving in us, to prepare for us the most precious jewels of Christ's body and blood. By these our ransom is fully paid, the law fulfilled, and his justice fully satisfied.

Christ is now the righteousness of all those who truly believe in him. He *for them* paid their ransom by his death. He *for them* fulfilled the law in his life. So that now, in him and by him, every true Christian may be called a fulfiller of the law.

Apply

Can you say in a sentence what part our good works have alongside faith?

Meditate on the fact that Jesus not only paid your ransom but also fulfilled the law in your place.

Pray

Praise God that he not only saves us by faith alone apart from works (Romans 3:28), but that even faith is a gift from him.

Thank Jesus for all he has done in your place: paying your ransom, fulfilling the law, and satisfying God's justice.

Notes and Prayers

✳ Day 10 ✳

For the Glory of Christ

Revelation 1:4–8

Justification by faith alone has always been the strong rock and foundation of Christian religion because it gives all glory to God.

Read Revelation 1:4–8

Why does John ascribe glory to Jesus in verses 5–6?

What will be the reaction of those who opposed Jesus, in verse 7?

Not a Novel Doctrine

Consider diligently these words: *without works, by faith only, freely, we receive remission of our sins*. What can be spoken more plainly than to say that freely, without works, by faith only, we obtain remission of our sins?

That we are justified by faith only, freely and without works, we do often read in the best and most ancient writers. Hilary of Poitiers says these words plainly: 'Faith alone justifies'. And Basil of Caesarea, a Greek author, writes that 'this is a perfect and a whole rejoicing in God, when a person acknowledges that they lack true justice and righteousness, and are justified only by faith in Christ'.

Beside Hilary, Basil, and Ambrose, we read the same in Origen, Chrysostom, Cyprian, Augustine, Prosper, Oecomenius, Photius, Bernardus, Anselm, and many other authors, Greek and Latin.

But this proposition – that we are justified by faith only, freely and without works – is spoken in order clearly to take away all merit of our works, as being insufficient to deserve our justification at God's hands. Thereby it most plainly expresses our weakness and the goodness of God, the great infirmity of ourselves and the might and power of God, the imperfection of our own works and the most abundant grace of our Saviour, Christ. And thereby wholly to ascribe the merit and deserving of our justification to Christ only and his most precious blood-shedding.

A Doctrine That Brings Glory to God

This faith the holy Scripture teaches. This is the strong rock and foundation of Christian religion. This doctrine all old and ancient authors of Christ's church do approve.

This doctrine advances and sets forth the true glory of Christ, and suppresses the vainglory of mankind. Whoever denies this is not to be thought of as a true Christian, nor for a setter forth of Christ's glory, but for an adversary of Christ and his gospel, and for a setter forth of mankind's vainglory.

Apply

Meditate on the idea that true, orthodox doctrine brings glory to Christ, whereas false doctrine exalts mankind at God's expense. Can you think of other examples of this?

The Reformers claimed to be rediscovering true doctrine rather than making it up afresh. How important do you think that is?

Pray

Praise God that all the glory for our salvation goes to him alone and not to us.

Ask God to help you give him all the glory in your life and in your doctrine.

Notes and Prayers

Day 11

Devilish Faith

James 2:14–26

Our duty is not to pass the time of this present life unfruitfully and idly, not caring how few good works we do to the glory of God and profit of our neighbours.

Read James 2:14–26

Is it possible for true faith (which alone justifies us) to remain idle?

What does James mean by the demons having faith / believing in God (verse 19)?

Orthodox but Unsaved

That faith which brings forth (without repentance) either evil works or no good works is not a right, pure and lively faith, but a dead, devilish and counterfeit faith. Even the devils know and believe that Christ suffered a most painful death for our sakes to redeem us from eternal death, and that he rose again from death on the third day. They believe that he ascended into heaven, and that he sits on the right hand of the Father, and at the last end of this world shall come again to judge both the living and the dead.

These articles of our faith, the devils believe, and so they believe all things that are written in the New and Old Testaments to be true. And yet for all this faith, they are but devils, remaining still in their damnable state, lacking the very true Christian faith.

True Faith

For the right and true Christian faith is not only to believe that holy Scripture and all the previously mentioned articles of our faith are true, but also to have a sure trust and confidence in God's merciful promises, to be saved from everlasting damnation by Christ. From this follows a loving heart to obey his commandments.

And this true Christian faith, no devil has – nor any human who, in the outward profession of their mouth, and in the outward receiving of the sacraments, in coming to church and in all other outward appearances, seems to be a Christian, and yet in their living and deeds shows the contrary.

For how can someone have this true faith, this sure trust and confidence in God – that by the merits of Christ their sins are cancelled and they are reconciled to the favour of God and are partakers of the kingdom of heaven by Christ – when they live ungodly lives and deny Christ in their deeds? Surely, no such ungodly person can have this faith and trust in God. For as they know Christ to be the only Saviour of the world, so they know also that wicked people shall not possess the kingdom of God.

Apply

Tremble that there is more orthodox theology in hell than in many palaces, pulpits and pews, and yet it does the demonic minions of Satan no spiritual good at all.

Are you orthodox in your head but not trusting in God's promises in your heart or life? Talk to someone you trust about any struggles you might have here.

Pray

Pray that you would truly trust and rely on Christ each day, and not merely appear to say and do the right things among Christian friends.

Pray for any you know who profess with their lips but do not live a biblically-defined godly life, that they would repent and not be excluded from God's kingdom.

Notes and prayers

Day 12

Pleasing God

Romans 8:5–11

Those who fantasise that they are set at liberty from doing all good works and may live as they please trifle with God and deceive themselves.

Read Romans 8:5–11

What does Paul mean, that the mind set on the flesh cannot please God (verse 8)?

Is it possible for a Christian to please God?

Living in Sin

Do not deceive yourselves, thinking that you have faith in God or that you love God or do trust in him or do fear him, when you live in sin. For then your ungodly and sinful life declares the contrary, whatever you may say or think.

It pertains to a Christian to have this true Christian faith, and to test themselves whether they have it or not, and to know what belongs to it, and how it works in them. A true faith cannot be kept secret, but when occasion is offered it will break out and show itself by good works. The soul that has a lively faith in it will always be doing some good work which shall declare that it is living, and will not be unoccupied.

Living Faith

Faith gives life to the soul, and those who lack faith are as dead to God as those who lack souls are dead to the world. Without faith, all that is done by us is but dead before God, although the work seems never so glorious before man.

Even as the picture engraved or painted is but a dead representation of the thing itself, and is without life or any manner of moving, so are the works of all unfaithful persons before God. They appear to be lively works, but truly they are but dead, not leading to eternal life. They are but shadows and shows of lively and good things, and not good and lively things indeed.

For true faith gives life to works, and out of such faith comes good works that are truly very good works; yet without it, no work is good before God. As Augustine says, we must not set good works before faith, nor think that before faith someone may do any good work. For such works, although they seem to other people to be praiseworthy, yet truly they are but vain, and not allowed before God. They are like the course of a horse that runs out of the set path, labouring hard but to no purpose.

Apply

If it is true that 'without faith it is impossible to please God' (Hebrews 11:6), how does God view the seemingly praiseworthy works of your non-Christian friends?

Does your own life match your profession of faith, or is your faith secret and inactive?

Pray

Pray that your non-Christian friends would not be like the horse running like crazy outside the set course, but would come to have faith in Christ to animate their works.

Ask God to give you a living faith, which spills out into good works and shows itself.

Notes and Prayers

✳ Day 13 ✳

The Works of True Faith

MATTHEW 19:16–22

True faith is never idle and without good works. And good works acceptable to God cannot be done without faith. But what kind of works should we do?

Read Matthew 19:16–22

Which of the Ten Commandments does Jesus not mention here?

Why do you think that is?

The Moral Commandments

What kind of works spring out of true faith, and lead faithful people to everlasting life? This can be best learned from our Saviour Christ himself, who was asked by a certain great man the same question. Jesus answered him, 'If you want to come to everlasting life, keep the commandments.' But the Scribes and Pharisees had made so many of their own laws and traditions, to bring people to heaven, besides God's commandments, that this man was in doubt about whether he should come to heaven by those laws and traditions or by the law of God, and therefore he asked Christ which commandments he meant.

Christ answered him plainly, rehearsing the commandments of God: 'You shall not kill. You shall not commit adultery. You shall not steal. You shall not bear false witness. Honour your father and your mother, and love your neighbour as yourself' (Matthew 19:18–19). By which words Christ declared that the laws of God are the very way that leads to everlasting life, and not the traditions and laws of people. So this is to be taken as a most true lesson taught by Christ's own mouth, that the works of the moral commandments of God are the very true works of faith, which lead to the blessed life to come.

Human Fantasies

But people's blindness and malice, even from the beginning, has always been ready to fall from God's commandments. Adam, the first man, had but one commandment, that he should not eat of the forbidden fruit. Despite God's commandment, he gave credit to the woman, seduced by the subtle persuasion of the serpent, and so followed his own will, and left God's commandment. And ever since that time, everyone who has come from him has been so blinded through original sin, that they have always been ready to fall from God and his law, and to invent a new way to salvation by works of their own devising. Such was the roughness of the people, after they fell to their own fantasies and left the eternal, living God and his commandments, that they devised innumerable images and gods.

Apply

Are there 'works of their own devising' that you are tempted to follow rather than the actual moral commandments of God?

Do you know the Ten Commandments which Jesus quotes from? Try to memorise them (see Exodus 20).

Pray

Thank God that his word itself is very clear about the moral commandments we are meant to follow, and does not leave us to devise our own morality.

Pray that with the help of the Holy Spirit you may be enabled to keep his commandments by faith.

Notes and prayers

❊ Day 14 ❊

Love Your Enemies

1 Peter 2:21–25

Christ taught about true love that everyone is bound to love God above all things, and to love every person – both friend and foe.

Read 1 Peter 2:21–25

What are the alternatives to suffering injustice in the way Christ did (verse 23)?

Why do we find it difficult to follow the command and example of Jesus to love our enemies?

Distinctively Christian Love

The perverse nature of mankind, corrupted with sin and destitute of God's word and grace, thinks it against all reason that someone should love their enemy, and in many ways is persuaded against this. Against all such reasons, we ought to set the teaching as well as the living of our Saviour Christ who, loving us when we were his enemies, teaches us to love our enemies. He patiently endured many reproaches for us, suffered beating, and most cruel death. Therefore, we are not members of him if we will not follow him. Christ, says St Peter, suffered for us, leaving an example that we should follow him (1 Peter 2:21).

Furthermore, we must consider that to love our friends is no more than thieves, adulterers, murderers, and all wicked people do. Jews, Muslims, non-believers, and even all brute beasts love those who are their friends, those from whom they earn their living, or get any other benefits. But to love enemies is the proper condition of those who are the children of God, the disciples and followers of Christ.

Forgiveness

The disobedient and corrupt nature of people ponders deeply and repeatedly the offence and displeasure done to them by their enemies, and thinks it an intolerable burden to be bound to love those who hate them. But the burden should be easy enough if (on the other side) everyone would consider what displeasure they have done to their enemy in return, and what pleasure they have received from this.

And let us ponder the displeasures which we have given to Almighty God, how often and how grievously we have offended him. If we wish to have God's forgiveness, there is no other remedy but to forgive the offences done to us, which are very small in comparison to our offences against God. And if we consider that the one who has offended us does not deserve to be forgiven by us, let us consider again that we deserve far less to be forgiven by God.

Apply

Ponder your own sins against God, and how big they are compared to the things people have done to you.

Is there someone you find it hard to love and forgive? What can you do about that issue in your own heart (even if you can't reconcile or solve the things that may have caused the relational breakdown)?

Pray

Pray the Lord's Prayer, with a particular emphasis on 'forgive us our sins, as we forgiven those who sin against us.'

Ask for God's strength to love those who won't love you back, and to show you appropriate ways to do so.

Notes and Prayers

✵ Day 15 ✵

Swearing Oaths

Matthew 5:33–37

When Christ so earnestly forbade swearing, it should not be understood as though he forbade all oaths. But he forbids all vain swearing.

Read Matthew 5:33–37

Can you imagine what kind of oaths the people were swearing in this passage, which Jesus forbids?

In what ways do people today use oaths and assertions of their honesty in conversation and business?

Lawful and Unlawful Oaths

Almighty God commanded that no one should take his name in their mouth vainly. He threatened punishment to those who irreverently abuse it by swearing, perjury, and blasphemy. So that this commandment may be better known and kept, it shall be declared to you both how it is lawful for Christian people to swear an oath, and also what peril and danger it is vainly to swear such oaths, or to commit perjury.

First, when judges require oaths of people for declaration of the truth or for execution of justice, this manner of swearing is lawful. But when people swear out of custom, in reasoning, buying and selling, or other daily communications, such swearing is ungodly, unlawful, and prohibited by the commandment of God. For such swearing is nothing else but the taking of God's holy name in vain.

Necessary and Unnecessary Oaths

God by the prophet Jeremiah says, 'You shall swear, 'The Lord lives', in truth, in judgment, in righteousness' (Jeremiah 4:2). So that whoever swears when they are required to by a judge, let them be sure in their conscience that their oath has these three conditions, and they shall never need to be afraid of perjury. The one who swears may swear *truly*, that is, they must have the truth only before their eyes. Second, the one who takes an oath must do it *with judgment*, not rashly and unadvisedly, but soberly, considering what an oath is. Thirdly, the one who swears must swear *in righteousness*, that is, for the very zeal and love which they have for righteousness of the matter or cause.

Perhaps some will say, 'I am compelled to swear, or else those who live with me, or buy and sell with me will not believe me.' But the one who uses truth and plainness in their bargaining and communication shall have no need of such vain swearing to make themselves credible with their neighbours. If their credence is really so lost that they think no one will believe them without such oaths, then they may well think that their credibility has completely gone.

Apply

You should have no qualms about taking oaths when required by a court of law. Can you think of other circumstances where you might be asked to make an oath in a Jeremiah 4:2 way?

Do you casually use (or hear) blasphemy or phrases which assert your truthfulness in conversation, which might be considered rash or unnecessary or ungodly? Maybe ask a friend to tell you if you do.

Pray

Ask God to show you where you might be taking his name in vain and not speaking with truth, judgment, and righteousness.

Pray that God would help you speak truthfully at all times.

Notes and prayers

✵ Day 16 ✵

Falling Away

Hosea 5:1–7

Turning away from God is a dangerous thing to do, because he may turn away from us as a result and leave us to our own sin and condemnation.

Read Hosea 5:1–7

What is stopping the people of Hosea's day from returning to God? (verses 4–5)

When does religion not work? (verses 6–7)

God Withdraws from Pride

A wise man said that pride was the first beginning of our falling away from God. For by it, our hearts are turned from God our maker. And as by pride and sin we go away from God, so shall God and all goodness with him go from us. The prophet Hosea plainly affirms that those who move away from God by living in vice, and yet would try to pacify him with sacrifices and satisfy him that way – they labour in vain. For, despite all their sacrifices, he will withdraw himself from them. For, says the prophet, they do not apply their minds to return to God; although they go about with whole flocks and herds to seek the Lord, yet they shall not find him, for he has withdrawn from them (Hosea 5:4–6).

Don't Test God's Patience

Nevertheless, God is so merciful, and so patient, that he does not bring upon us that great wrath suddenly. But when we begin to shrink from his word, not believing it or not expressing it in our lives, first he sends his messengers, the true preachers of his word, to admonish and warn us of our duty. And if this does not work, but we still remain disobedient to his word and will – then he warns us by terrible threatenings that whoever does these works shall never enter into his rest, which is the kingdom of heaven (Hebrews 4:1–13. Galatians 5:21. Psalm 95:11).

Those who do not live for God in this world, but for their own carnal liberty, do not perceive this great wrath of God towards them, that he leaves them alone even to themselves. But God forbid that we should ever desire such liberty. For although God sometimes allows the wicked to have their pleasure in this world, yet the final end of ungodly living is eventually endless destruction.

Nothing should pierce our heart so much, and make us feel so horribly afraid, as when we know in our conscience that we have grievously offended God, and continue to do so, and yet he strikes us not, but quietly allows us to continue in the wickedness that we delight in.

Apply

What's the difference between true repentance that returns to God, and the kind of ineffective religion that Hosea described?

Don't test God's patience – if he is warning you and teaching you about some sin in your life, go back to him now and repent. Don't wait for him to go away.

Pray

Ask God to grant you repentance and a knowledge of the truth (2 Timothy 2:25–26) so you can always return to him when you sin.

Pray for those you know who have fallen away from true faith in God. That he would be merciful towards them, speak to them from his word, and bring them back.

Notes and Prayers

�֍ Day 17 ✶

No Fear in Death

John 6:35–51

Every Christian perceives by the infallible word of God that bodily death cannot harm or hinder those who truly believe in Christ.

Read John 6:35–51

What things does Jesus promise to those who look to him and believe in him?

Why might we still be afraid of dying?

The Fear of Death

There are three causes why worldly people fear death. One, because they shall lose their worldly honours, riches, possessions, and all their heart's desires when they die. Second, because of the painful diseases and bitter pangs which people commonly suffer either before or at the time of death. But the main cause above all others is the dread of that miserable state of eternal damnation both of body and soul, which they fear shall follow after they depart out of the worldly pleasures of this present life.

Deliverance from Fear

But – everlasting thanks be to Almighty God for ever! – there is never one of all these causes, no, nor all of them together, that can make a true Christian afraid to die – since they are truly members of Christ, the temple of the Holy Spirit, the children of God and true inheritors of the everlasting kingdom of heaven. On the contrary, they can see a great many causes, undoubtedly grounded upon the infallible and everlasting truth of the word of God, which move them to put away the fear of bodily death. They may even wish, desire, and heartily long for it, because of the manifold benefits and remarkable advantages which follow for every faithful person.

For death shall be to them no death at all, but truly a deliverance from death, and from all the pains, cares, and sorrows, miseries, and wretchedness of this world. It will truly be an entrance into rest, and a beginning of everlasting joy.

So although we have our souls separated from our bodies for a season, yet at the general resurrection we shall be more fresh, beautiful, and perfect than we are now. For now we are mortal, but then we shall be immortal. Now we are infected with various infirmities, but then we shall be completely free of all mortal infirmities. Now we are subject to all carnal desires, but then we shall be entirely spiritual, desiring nothing except God's glory and things eternal.

Apply

Are you afraid to die? Do you experience any of the three causes of fear outlined here? How does the gospel help?

Reflect on all the good things which death will bring to you, if you believe and trust in Jesus.

Pray

Praise God that he will raise us up if we trust in Jesus, and that we will be 'more fresh, beautiful, and perfect than we are now' on that day.

Pray that God would calm your fears and help you so focus on Jesus that the things of this world would become less important to you (honours, riches, possessions etc).

Notes and Prayers

✳ Day 18 ✳

Obey the Authorities

Romans 13:1–7

Let us, as subjects and citizens, do our bounden duties, giving hearty thanks to God and praying for the preservation of godly order in our societies.

Read Romans 13:1–7

Why does Paul say we should obey the authorities set over us?

What is the proper role of such authorities?

Godly Order

Take away kings, rulers, magistrates, judges, and such divinely-ordained roles, and no one could travel or move about without being robbed, or sleep in their own house or bed without being murdered. No one could keep their wife, children, or possessions safe. All things would be common and there would necessarily follow all mischief and utter destruction, both of souls, bodies, goods, and commonwealths.

Let us consider the Scriptures of the Holy Spirit, which persuade and command us all to be obedient. Here let us all learn from St Paul, the chosen instrument of God (Acts 9:15), that all people having souls owe a duty, even in conscience, obedience, submission, and subjection to the high powers which are constituted in authority by God. For they are ordained by God himself, from whom alone they have all their power and all their authority. And the same St Paul threatens nothing less than everlasting damnation to all disobedient people, to all those who resist this general and common authority. For they resist not people, but God; not a human design or invention, but God's wisdom, God's order, power, and authority.

Rebellion and Disobedience

Our saviour Christ himself, and his apostles, received many and various injuries from unfaithful and wicked people in authority; yet we never read that any of them caused any sedition or rebellion against authority. We often read that they patiently suffered all troubles, vexations, slanders, pangs, and pains, and death itself obediently, without disorder or resistance. They committed their cause to him who judges righteously (1 Peter 2:23), and prayed for their enemies heartily and earnestly. They knew that the authority of the powers that be was God's ordinance, and therefore both in their words and deeds they always taught obedience to it, and never taught or did the opposite.

However, let us undoubtedly believe that we may not obey rulers, magistrates, or any other authority – even our own fathers – if they command us to do anything contrary to God's commandments. In such a case, we ought to say with the apostles, 'We must obey God, rather than human beings' (Acts 5:29).

Apply

What rules and laws of the society you live in might you be tempted to disobey? How should Christians think about such acts of disobedience?

What situations can you foresee where it might be necessary for you as a Christian to disobey the state because it commands something contrary to God's law? How can you prepare for that?

Pray

Thank God for the good order in your society (as much as you are able to).

Ask God to deliver you from the evil of having to choose to disobey because the state demands something contrary to his own law. And for strength to do so if necessary.

Notes and prayers

✳ Day 19 ✳

Flee Sexual Sin

1 Corinthians 6:12–20

To avoid sexual sin, let us ensure that we keep our hearts pure and clean from all evil thoughts and carnal lusts. For if our heart is so infected and corrupted, we fall headlong into all kinds of ungodliness.

Read 1 Corinthians 6:12–20

How does Paul say we should think about our bodies, as Christians?

Why does he say sexual immorality is a bad thing?

Unlawful Use

If you call to mind this commandment of God – 'You shall not commit adultery' – you will perceive that fornication and promiscuity are most abominable sins in the sight of God. The word 'adultery' properly means the unlawful joining together of a married man with any woman except his wife, or of a wife with any man except her husband. Yet it also signifies all unlawful use of those body parts which are set apart for procreation. And this one commandment forbidding adultery, sufficiently paints the picture before our eyes of the greatness of this sin of sexual immorality, and clearly declares how greatly it should be abhorred by all honest and faithful people. None of us should think of themselves as excepted from this commandment, whether we are old or young, married or unmarried, man or woman.

Avoiding Defilement

Jesus said, 'out of the heart come evil thoughts, murder, adultery, sexual immorality, theft, false witness, blasphemy. These are the things which defile a person' (Matthew 15:1–20). Here we may see that not only murder, theft, false witness, and blasphemy defile someone; but also evil thoughts, adultery, fornication, and sexual immorality. Therefore, who is so stupid that they will consider sexual immorality and fornication to be things of small importance and of no weight before God? How can it be anything else but a most abominable sin, seeing that it must not even be named among Christians, much less in any way be committed (Ephesians 5:3)?

It would be good also for us to always live in the fear of God and to set before our eyes the grievous threatenings of God against all ungodly sinners. And we should consider in our minds how impure, carnal, and brief that pleasure is to which Satan moves us. And again, how the pain appointed as punishment for that sin is intolerable and everlasting. Moreover, we must be moderate and sober in eating and drinking, avoid unclean conversation, avoid all immoral company, flee idleness, delight in reading holy scripture, and watch in godly prayers and virtuous meditations.

Apply

The Homily also says sexual sin is often considered no sin at all – 'not rebuked but winked at, not punished but laughed at.' Considering all the reasons given above for why it is a terrible thing (count them!), why do people today think so lightly of this sin?

It also says, 'if, when we feel inwardly that Satan our old enemy tempts us to sexual immorality, we by no means consent to his crafty suggestions but valiantly resist and withstand him by strong faith in the word of God.' Have you been doing that? How can you do so more effectively?

Pray

Pray that God would enable you by his Spirit who lives in you, to honour him in your body (1 Corinthians 6:20). Confess your failures to do so always.

Ask that God would not let your mind be deceived by the world, the flesh, or the devil into thinking less seriously of sexual sin (Ephesians 5:6).

Notes and Prayers

✳ Day 20 ✳

Contention

2 Timothy 2:16–26

When it comes to speaking evil against other people – first, let us examine ourselves, whether we are faultless and clear of the fault which we find in others.

Read 2 Timothy 2:16–26

What is wrong with 'godless chatter' or 'foolish and stupid arguments'?

What is the opposite of being quarrelsome?

Hot Words

Among all kinds of contention, none is more hurtful than contention in matters of religion. 'Have nothing to do with foolish, ignorant controversies,' says St Paul, 'because you know that they breed quarrels. The servant of God must not be quarrelsome but kind to everyone' (2 Timothy 2:23–24; 1 Timothy 1:4). For there are too many people, in alehouses or other places, who delight to argue about certain questions, not so as to build people up in the truth but for vain glory, and showing off their cunning. And so un-soberly do they reason and dispute that when neither party will give place to the other they fall to criticism and contention, and sometimes from hot words to further improper behaviour.

True Strength

Let us so read the scripture that by reading it we may be made better livers, rather than more contentious disputers. If anything is necessary to be taught, reasoned, or disputed, let us do it with all meekness, softness, and gentleness. If anything happens to be spoken disagreeably, let one bear another's frailty. Let those who are at fault rather amend than defend that which they have spoken amiss, in case they fall by contention from a foolish error into an obstinate heresy. For it is better, to give way meekly than to win the victory with a breach of love – which is what happens when everyone defends their opinion obstinately.

The one who cannot temper or rule their own anger is weak and feeble, and not a strong person. For true strength is to overcome wrath and to think little of injury and other people's foolishness. Those who wish to excuse their own impatience find many pretences to do so. 'My enemy,' they say, 'is not worthy to have gentle words or deeds, being so full of malice and argumentativeness.' The less they are worthy, the more you are encouraged by God, the more you are commended by Christ (for whose sake you should render good for evil), because he has commanded you and also deserves your obedience in this.

Apply

Are you ever stubborn and 'un-soberly' in the way you debate with people? (Maybe ask a friend to tell you if you are.) How can you prevent yourself engaging in that way?

How can you ensure that all your words aim to 'build people up in the truth' and show love rather than malice?

Pray

Ask the Holy Spirit to reveal to you when and where you may have been too contentious in disputes. Pray for forgiveness and an opportunity to make amends.

Pray that God would make you a better liver of the truth, rather than a more contentious disputer, so you will not become more and more ungodly and lead people astray.

Notes and prayers

The First Book of Homilies

HOMILIES

The Church of England's Official Sermons in Modern English

The Homilies were originally published in 1547, to help reform and renew the Church of England in the biblical faith of the Reformation. They unfold the doctrines of scripture, sin, salvation, and Christian living with clarity and verve. This is what makes returning to the Homilies—now, for the first time, updated in modern English—such an invigorating and life-giving thing to do today.

"The dreadful ignorance as to the fundamentals of our holy religion, that almost everywhere abounds amongst the members of our established church, is chiefly owing to our neglect of preaching and putting into their hands the grand doctrines of the Reformation, contained in these Homilies." George Whitefield (1714-1770)

"The Homilies are a pattern of simplicity and godly sincerity. In their mode of stating divine truth, and enforcing it upon the conscience, they never have been excelled by any composition whatever." Charles Simeon (1759-1836)

"Here we have up-to-date language and inspirational content. I commend this book to you as being challenging, educational, readable, relevant, and necessary for all serious Anglicans throughout the world." Bishop Henry Scriven

£15 hardback, £10 paperback, £5 digital;
UK orders direct from Church Society see:
www.churchsociety.org
admin@churchsociety.org | +44 1923 255410

ISBN: 978-1-7399376-0-7

A Month with the Messiah
Reflections on Handel's Masterpiece

Handel's Messiah has captivated audiences for centuries, but the depth of its theological and spiritual messages invites deeper exploration. In A Month with the Messiah, a cast of thirty scholars, pastors, musicians, and theologians come together to provide a profound and accessible devotional commentary on this musical masterpiece. Curated to appeal both to long-time admirers and newcomers, this book dives into the libretto's scriptural themes with clarity and reverence.

This beautifully produced hardback companion to the Messiah invites readers on a journey of spiritual reflection, exploring the hope, redemption, and joy that Handel's music captures so vividly. Each contributor brings a unique perspective, drawing from their rich backgrounds to shed light on how these passages resonate in today's world.

Whether you're enjoying Messiah for the first time or looking to deepen your appreciation of it, this collection is a companion to enrich your listening, worship, and reflection on Handel's enduring work.

Perfect as a book for Advent, as a Christmas gift for someone else, or for your own enjoyment!

£14.99 Hardback, £9.99 digital

Order direct from Church Society:

www.churchsociety.org | admin@churchsociety.org
+44 1923 255410

Church Society

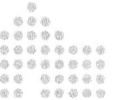

Church Society

offering strategic leadership

For more than 180 years, Church Society has been contending to reform and renew the Church of England in biblical faith, on the basis of its Reformed foundations as expressed in the doctrine of the Articles, the worship of the Prayer Book, and the ministry of the Ordinal.

To find out more and to join Church Society, please visit our website, churchsociety.org

resourcing today's church

Church Society publishes several new books each year, bringing the best of our Anglican Evangelical heritage to new generations, and responding to new pressures and opportunities in today's Church and nation. We also produce a weekly podcast, a quarterly magazine and a theological journal, as well as our regular blog.

serving tomorrow's church

As part of our commitment to raising up a new generation of leaders, we host the annual Junior Anglican Evangelical Conference for those in the early stages of ministry. Church Society also has patronage of around 130 parishes, helping to protect evangelical ministry in the Church of England for the future.

www.ingramcontent.com/pod-product-compliance
Lightning Source LLC
Chambersburg PA
CBHW040246010526
44119CB00057B/834